CARS

100 YEARS AGO

by Allison Lassieur

amicus readers

2

amicus readers

Say hello to amicus readers.

You'll find our helpful dog, Amicus, chasing a ball—to let you know the reading level of a book.

A

Learn to Read

Frequent repetition of sentence structures, high frequency words, and familiar topics provide ample support for brand new readers. Approximately 100 words.

1

Read Independently

Repetition is mixed with varied sentence structures and 6 to 8 content words per book are introduced with photo label and picture glossary supports. Approximately 150 words.

2

Read to Know More

These books feature a higher text load with additional nonfiction features such as more photos, time lines, and text divided into sections. Approximately 250 words.

Amicus Readers are published by **Amicus**
P.O. Box 1329, Mankato, Minnesota 56002
www.amicuspublishing.us

U.S. publication copyright © 2012 Amicus.
International copyright reserved in all countries.
No part of this book may be reproduced in any
form without written permission from the publisher.

Printed in the United States of America at Corporate
Graphics, in North Mankato, Minnesota.

Series Editor   Rebecca Glaser
Series Designer   Heather Dreisbach
Photo Researcher   Heather Dreisbach

Library of Congress Cataloging-in-Publication Data
Lassieur, Allison.
  Cars : 100 years ago / by Allison Lassieur.
    p. cm. – (Amicus Readers. 100 years ago)
  Includes index.
  Summary: "Discusses turn-of-the-century cars and how
they are different from the early 1900s to today. Includes
"What's Different?" photo quiz"–Provided
by publisher.
  ISBN 978-1-60753-161-6 (library binding)
  1. Automobiles–History–Juvenile literature. I. Title.
TL206.L37 2012
629.222–dc22
                                          2010039114

Photo Credits
Archive Pics/Alamy, 15, 21m; Bettmann/CORBIS, 18; Car Culture/Getty Images, 8, 20m; CORBIS, 5, 22t; emin
kuliyev/Shutterstock, 22b; Getty Images , 13; Hulton Collection/Getty Images, 10, 20b; O. C. HAVENS/National
Geographic Stock, 17; PEMCO-Webster & Stevens Collection; Museum of History and Industry, Seattle/CORBIS,
16; Photolibrary/National Motor Museum, 6, 12, 20t; The Granger Collection, NYC—All rights reserved, 14; The
Print Collector/Alamy, 9, 21b; Vintage Image/Alamy, cover, 1, 11, 21t

1024   3-2011
10 9 8 7 6 5 4 3 2 1

TABLE OF CONTENTS

Cars: A New Idea

About one hundred years ago, many people still used horses and carriages to travel. This kind of travel took a long time. Most people didn't travel far from their homes. Cars were a new idea.

No one knew what to call these new machines. So people called them horseless carriages. Later they were called automobiles and cars.

What Made Cars Run?

Inventors built different kinds of cars. But the cars had problems. Electric cars were beautiful. But they cost a lot.

ELECTRIC CAR

STEAM-ENGINE CAR

Steam-engine cars were cheap to run.

But they sometimes blew up!

9

Gasoline-powered cars were fast and easy to use. People liked gasoline-powered cars the best.

Gasoline was cheap to buy. One gallon of gas only cost a quarter.

DRIVING A CAR

Many cars didn't have roofs or
windows. Dust, dirt, and rain got in.

People wore driving clothes like hats, goggles, and long white coats called dusters. The clothes helped them stay clean and dry.

FORD MOTOR CARS

Illustrating
Four Posi-
tions of the
Model T
Touring Car
with Top

Serviceable
and of very
pleasing ap-
pearance
from every
view point

WATCH THE FORDS GO BY

Most people didn't have enough money to buy a car. In 1908, a man named Henry Ford invented the Model T. It was sturdy and inexpensive. A Model T cost about $850. Now almost everyone could own a car.

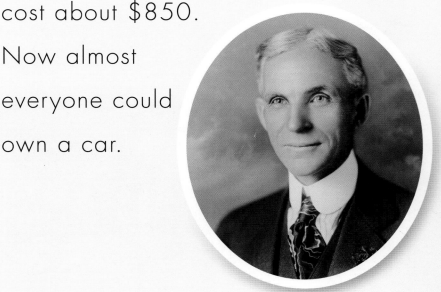

HENRY FORD

WHERE DID CARS TRAVEL?

Driving wasn't always fun. Roads were made of dirt and rocks. In many places, there were no roads.

Cars got stuck in the mud.
There were no bridges. People
drove through creeks and rivers.

Cars allowed people to go places they'd never seen before. People drove to the tops of mountains. They drove to the edge of cliffs. They even drove into the sea! Cars changed the way people traveled.

PHOTO GLOSSARY

duster—a long coat worn by people riding in cars

electric car—a car that runs on electricity; electric cars were started with a crank.

gasoline car—a car that uses liquid gas for fuel

horseless carriage—a four-wheeled vehicle with an engine

inventor—a person who thinks up and creates something new

steam engine—an engine powered by steam, which is created by burning wood or coal to heat water

WHAT'S DIFFERENT?

How many differences can you find between the street scene from 1910 and the street scene from today?

Ideas for Parents and Teachers

100 Years Ago, an Amicus Readers Level 2 series, introduces children to everyday life in the early 1900s. Use the following strategies to help readers predict and comprehend the text.

amicus readers

Before Reading
- Ask the child about cars.
- Have him or her describe how cars are a part of daily life.
- Ask about the differences between old and new cars.

Read the Book
- Read the book to the child, or have her read it independently.
- Point out details in the photos that are interesting or different from the cars that the child is familiar with.
- Show the child how to interpret the photos and how the images relate to the text.

After Reading
- Have the child explain the similarities and differences between cars one hundred years ago and today.
- Encourage the child to think further by asking questions such as, "How do you think it would feel to drive in a car then?" and "What kinds of things would you see if you drove through the country or the city?"

INDEX

WEB SITES

Henry Ford Museum
http://www.hfmgv.org/

Old Cars and Trucks
http://oldcarandtruckpictures.com/ModelTFord/

PBS Kids: Way Back Tech: Cars
http://www.pbskids.org/wayback/tech1900/car.html